Saturday Morning Cartoon

Drawing Activity Book

COLORING, DRAWING & ACTIVITY BOOKS
FOR ADULTS

Copyright 2016

All Rights reserved. No part of this book may be reproduced or used in any way or formor by any means whether electronic or mechanical, this means that you cannot recordor photocopy any material ideas or tips that are provided in this book.

How to use the book

. . .

Copy the simple steps on the blank page to learn how to draw the animal or object!

DRAW
THE
IMAGE

Sketch Here

Sketch Here

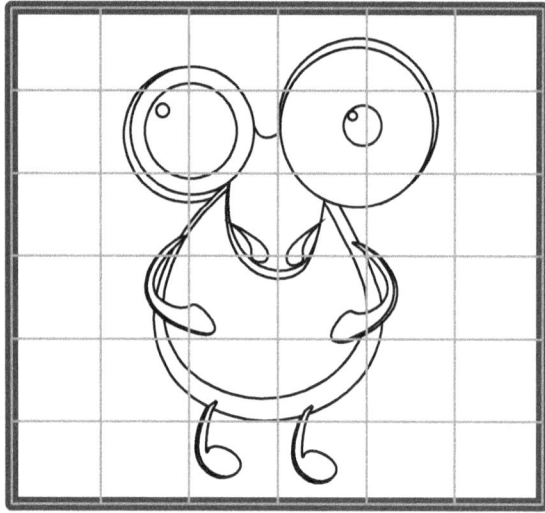

DRAW
THE
IMAGE

Sketch Here

Sketch Here

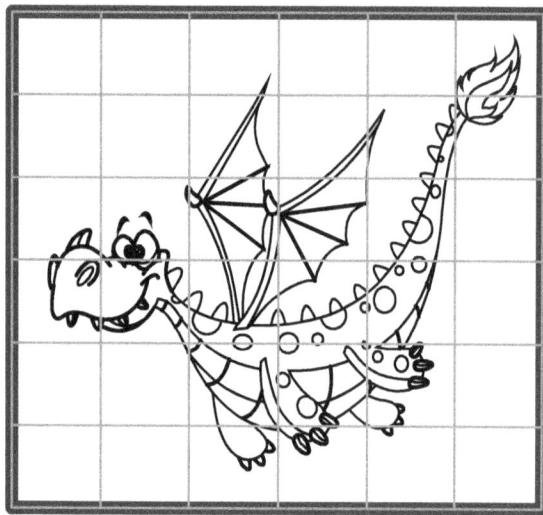

DRAW
THE
IMAGE

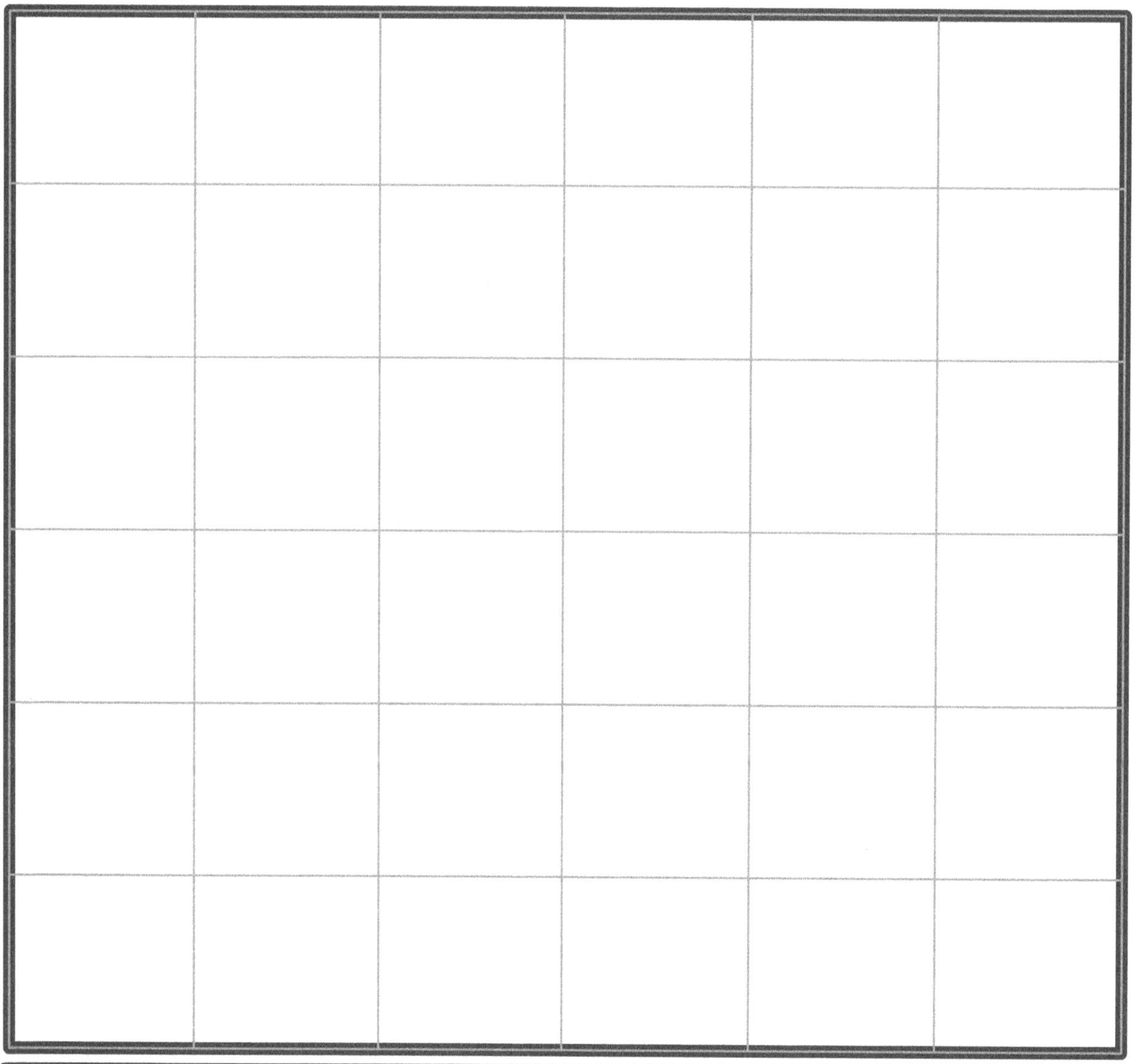

Sketch Here

DRAW
THE
IMAGE

Sketch Here

Sketch Here

DRAW
THE
IMAGE

Sketch Here

Sketch Here

DRAW
THE
IMAGE

Sketch Here

DRAW
THE
IMAGE

Sketch Here

DRAW
THE
IMAGE

Sketch Here

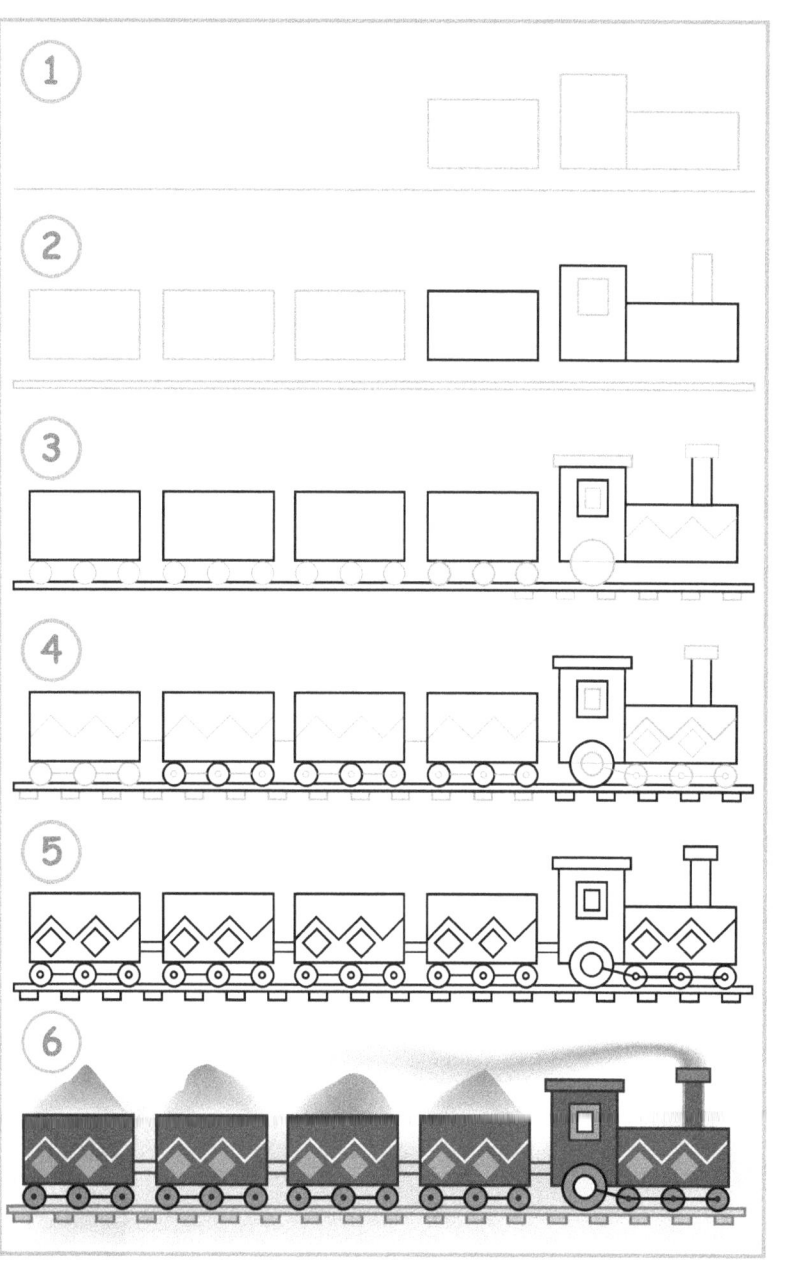

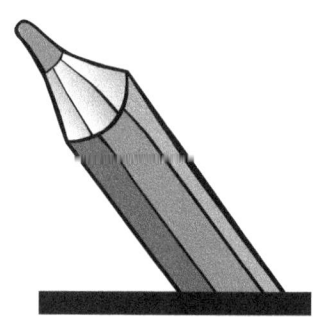

Sketch Here

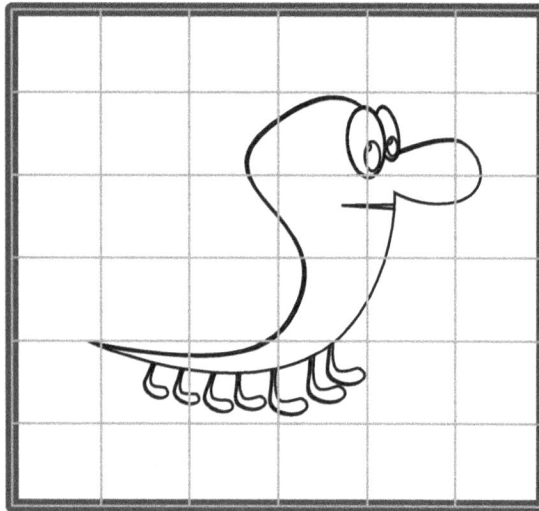

DRAW
THE
IMAGE

Sketch Here

DRAW
THE
IMAGE

Sketch Here

Sketch Here

DRAW
THE
IMAGE

Sketch Here

DRAW
THE
IMAGE

Sketch Here

www.ingramcontent.com/pod-product-compliance
Lightning Source LLC
LaVergne TN
LVHW061325060426
835507LV00019B/2297